THE CARNIVAL OF THE ANIMALS

WORCESTERSHIRE COUNTY
COUNCIL

604

Bertrams   28.01.06

£10.99

RE

THE CARNIVAL OF THE ANIMALS

POEMS INSPIRED BY SAINT-SAËNS' MUSIC
by
James Berry
Kit Wright
Cicely Herbert
Judith Chernaik
Adrian Mitchell
Gavin Ewart
X. J. Kennedy
Gerard Benson
Gillian Clarke
Valerie Bloom
Wendy Cope
Edwin Morgan
Charles Causley

ILLUSTRATED BY SATOSHI KITAMURA

WALKER BOOKS
AND SUBSIDIARIES

LONDON · BOSTON · SYDNEY · AUCKLAND

LION

Body colour of hay, big cat,
staring with fearless look.
Wild beast outdoing all
eagles flying, whales swimming.

Hunger switches you on, big cat.
Tiptoe breaks into trot, then
into athletic dash. You flash
dagger claws and crusher jaws
to hug a deer and pull it down,
grab it and tear it.

Oh what a love for meat, big cat,
what a show of speed and strength,
what an obsession with devouring.

Your only companions are lions, big cat.
You scorn all other creatures.
Vermin and flies travel with you,
night sky carries your quaking roars.

You yawn, roll over, unsheathe your claws.
Do your good looks, your mane of hair,
conceal your loneliness?

JAMES BERRY

COCKS AND HENS

You will never ever
Get away, get away,
Never ever get away
From me,
Though you flee!
(So sang the cock or rooster.)
You're just my image-booster,
Each one of you, and that is all
That you will ever be!

So he crowed to the hens
    As he chased them round the yard,
And the hens didn't like it,
    No, the hens took it hard.

        And they squeaked "Rot his beak!"
        And they squawked "He's all talk!
        He thinks he can fly
        Like an eagle or a hawk,
        But he's just a feathered fathead
        With a very silly walk!"

                    KIT WRIGHT

HORSES OF TARTARY

We're the wild bunch
faster than wind

little mobsters, fighters,
red-eyed, foam-flecked

hear the hooves pound
see the dust swirl

the streak of our manes
as we beat up the miles

smell the excitement
damp sweat of our skins

as we master our masters
we blow up a sandstorm

we thunder, we batter
we conquer the plains

CICELY HERBERT

TORTOISE

Under the mottled shell of the old tortoise
beats the heart of a young dancer.

She dreams of twirling on table-tops,
turning cartwheels,
kicking up her heels at the Carnival ball.

"Oh, who will kiss my cold and wrinkled lips,
and set my dreaming spirit free?"

JUDITH CHERNAIK

ELEPHANT ETERNITY

Elephants walking under juicy-leaf trees
Walking with their children under juicy-leaf trees
Elephants elephants walking like time

Elephants bathing in the foam-floody river
Fountaining their children in the mothery river
Elephants elephants bathing like happiness

Strong and gentle elephants
Standing on the earth
Strong and gentle elephants
Like peace

Time is walking under elephant trees
Happiness is bathing in the elephant river
Strong gentle peace is shining
All over the elephant earth

ADRIAN MITCHELL

KANGAROOS

Up and down! Up and down!
Kangaroos are jumping along,
clumping along,
thumping along,
all over town!

Up and down! Up and down!
Kangaroos are hopping along,
popping along,
clopping along,
all over town!

Up and down! Up and down!
Kangaroos are tripping along,
flipping along,
dipping along,
all over town!

Gavin Ewart

AQUARIUM

Flashes of fishes, quick flicks of tails.

Scoot scurry scamper of scattering scales.

A sponge blows bubbles, sea horses race,

Anemones wave tentacles of slow pink lace.

A whale of a sailfish unfolds a fin,

Fans a whiskery walrus with a double chin.

A shovelhead shark grins, his mouth underneath

Like a cave full of stalactites – steel-knife teeth.

The ocean brims over with creatures, it seems,

That swim past my eyes like remembered dreams.

From behind glass, a couple of curious squid

Stare out at me: *What's that odd thing – a kid?*

X. J. KENNEDY

PERSONAGES WITH LONG EARS

They wear large shoes and thick grey coats,
And occupy the ends of rows:
They sagely nod, and thus present
   The air of One Who Knows.

They scribble notes in scruffy pads,
And when the band begins to play,
They waggle those stupendous ears,
   Open their mouths – and bray.

     Yeee-haw! Yeeee-haw!! Yeeeee-haw!!!
     YEEEEEEEEEEE-HAW!!!!

GERARD BENSON

CUCKOO

Suddenly, under the sun's widening eye,
two notes from half a mile away.

Listen! Again! A sound so far, so deep
in trees waking their giant bones from sleep.

Two clear notes across the valley's well.
C and A flat like a distant bell.

We set our tools aside and listen hard
to hear it calling from the leafless wood,

thrilled once more to hear this summer guest
who pitches camp in a small bird's plundered nest,

grows fat on murder, and in a stolen house
sings her two notes in an angel's voice.

GILLIAN CLARKE

THE AVIARY

The signal comes and all at once,
The birds begin their aerial dance:
Swifts and swallows, tits, peafowls,
Mews and curlews, pipits, owls,
Starlings, sparrows, whippoorwills,
Merles and orioles, razorbills.

Birds of every size and hue
Skim swift as thought towards the blue,
They stop as one, turn and swoop
Earthward, float, and loop the loop,
Then spiral heavenwards again,
To form a feathered daisy-chain.

Below, the ostrich and her chicks
Follow the gyring aerobatics,
Drum counterpoint to the dulcet fluting,
Till like a host of parachuting
Painted balls they drop to perch
On walls, on branch of ash and birch.

VALERIE BLOOM

PIANISTS

Now, children, this fine animal is called the pianist.
One day he will delight us all with Chopin or with Liszt.

Perhaps. But there's a price to pay. Sometimes he feels quite sad
As he regales our ears with scales, knowing it drives us mad.

Look, two of them! Keep very quiet. They are concentrating.
The pianist doesn't bite, but interruptions are frustrating.

Can you give them sugar lumps? No, children, I think not.
Just wait until you're sure they've finished, then applaud a lot.

They'll bow and smile and smile and bow, and if you shout 'Encore!'
We'll have to stay a little longer, while they play some more.

Wendy Cope

FOSSILS

Dinosaur egg! Dinosaur egg!
We'll hatch you yet. Say please! Beg!

Jurassic Park! Jurassic Park!
Watch their jaws shine in the dark!

Iguanodon! Iguanodon!
Shambles erect in the London dawn.

Triceratops! Triceratops!
Rattles his bones until he drops.

Tyrannosaurus! Tyrannosaurus!
REX REX REX is all his chorus.

Where shall we find you, animals all?
You'll hear us roaring at the Carnival!

EDWIN MORGAN

THE SWAN

It is a music of the eye. The swan

Assumes the heavy garment of the stream

Among the sallow flags, the river grass;

Quite soundlessly as if within a dream

Moves through the secret light, gazes down on

Its perfect form as in a looking-glass.

Charles Causley

FINALE

Now they all perform together,
Fin and bone and fur and feather,
All in one glorious cavalcade —
The final Carnival Parade!

Gerard Benson

Over a hundred years ago, the French composer Camille Saint-Saëns dashed off a light-hearted 'zoological fantasy', musical pictures of animals dancing to popular songs and famous tunes – a surprise gift for a cellist friend. The composer was afraid *The Carnival of the Animals* was too frivolous to publish during his lifetime, except for the beautiful cello solo representing the swan. How amazed he would be today to learn that his Carnival is an all-time favourite of music lovers – and animal lovers – of all ages.

We asked several poets to write a poem for each animal, and this book, with Satoshi Kitamura's inspired illustrations, is the result. We hope you enjoy the new Carnival as much as we enjoyed making it.

Gerard Benson, Judith Chernaik and Cicely Herbert, Poems on the Underground

First published 2005 by Walker Books Ltd
87 Vauxhall Walk, London SE11 5HJ

2 4 6 8 10 9 7 5 3 1

Individual poems © 2005 individual poets
Illustrations © 2005 Satoshi Kitamura
Anthology © 2005 Poems on the Underground

The rights of the authors of the works comprising this anthology and the right of Satoshi Kitamura respectively have been asserted by them in accordance with the Copyright, Designs and Patents Act 1988

Printed in China

All rights reserved. No part of this book may be reproduced, transmitted or stored in an information retrieval system in any form or by any means, graphic, electronic or mechanical, including photocopying, taping and recording, without prior written permission from the publisher.

British Library Cataloguing in Publication Data:
a catalogue record for this book is available from the British Library

ISBN 1-84428-021-7

www.walkerbooks.co.uk